Rottens, Chatterboxes & Mayors

Rottens, Chatterboxes & Mayors

Three short plays from the Spanish Golden Age

Translated by

Catalina Castillón
Andy Coughlan

LITERARY PRESS
LAMAR UNIVERSITY

ISBN: 978-1-942956-34-1
Library of Congress Control Number: 2016951464

Cover and interior artwork: Andy Coughlan
Manufactured in the United States

Lamar University Literary Press
Beaumont, Texas

For
K.D. and R.Y.,
our families and friends,
and the global theater community

Other Lamar books you might enjoy

David Bowles, *Border Lore*
Kevin Casey, *Four Peace*
Terry Dalrymple, *Love Stories, Sort Of*
Gerald Duff, *Memphis Mojo*
Ted L. Estess, *Fishing Spirit Lake*
Gretchen Johnson, *The Joy of Deception*
Tom Mack and Andrew Geyer, editors, *A Shared Voice*
Jeanetta Calhoun Mish, *Oklahomeland*
Harold Raley, *Louisiana Rogue*
Jim Sanderson, *Trashy Behavior*
Jim Sanderson, *Sanderson's Fiction Writing Manual*
Jan Seale, *Appearances*
Steven Schroeder, *What's Love Got to Do With It? A city out of thin air*
Melvin Sterne, *The Number You Have Reached*
John Wegner, *Love is not a Dirty Word and Other Stories*
Robert Wexelblatt, *The Artist Wears Rough Clothing*

For information on these and other Lamar University
Literary Press books, go to
www.lamar.edu/literarypress

Acknowledgments

We are grateful to Miguel de Cervantes, Diego Velazquez and all the writers and artists of the Spanish Golden Age for their timeless contribution to the humanities. Four centuries later, their works still resonate.

CONTENTS

Introduction

The three plays that comprise this volume were chosen because they deal with timeless important issues, because they have the potential for a diverse cast, and because, probably most importantly, they are funny. Even though the plays were written 400 years ago, during the Spanish Golden Age, they still resonate with a modern audience as they deal with the basic foibles of the human condition.

They were also chosen to expose, through performance and interpretation, actors, audiences and readers to the works of the Spanish Golden Age, a period that is grossly underrepresented in English translations. The Spanish Golden Age is known in Spain as the *Siglo de oro* (The Golden Century), even though it encompasses more than 100 years. Historians consider the Spanish Golden Age to begin around 1516, when the Holy Roman Emperor Charles I of Spain—Charles V of Germany—took the throne, and runs through the end of the 17th century. Under the reign of Philip II (1555-1598), the politics and economy of Spain began to decline. However, this period began to see a flourishing of the arts, which continued through the 17th century. Miguel de

Cervantes Saavedra (1547-1616) perhaps epitomizes the Spanish Golden Age more than any other. However, Cervantes is not only the author of what is considered the first great novel, *Don Quixote*, he also wrote other novels, poetry and plays. Cervantes' short plays, also known as *entremeses*, are great examples of the genre.

An *entremés* is usually a one-act farce that could be in prose but was mostly in verse, which was often sung. Prose *entremeses* usually added music and songs near their conclusion. These interludes were presented between acts of the main play. They were usually humorous or bawdy, and they served to counter the main production as a comic relief (especially when the main play was serious or religious in nature). Frequently, the interludes commented on the main *comedia* which usually dealt with history, mythology or religion. In fact, some characters from the main play occasionally appeared in the *entremés*. These short plays often represented a common setting that was familiar to the ordinary folk among the audience. Many of these plays include social critiques; and, as in the case of these three plays, they represented absurd situations that satirized mundane obstacles of day-to-day existence.

The three plays in this collection are a great representation of Spanish Golden Age *entremeses*. Only one of them, *The Election of the Mayors of*

Daganzo (La elección de los Alcades de Daganzo), was published under Cervantes' name, while the other two are tentatively attributed to him. Reading the plays, one can see similarities in the texts—both in style and in humor—that lead one to believe they come from Cervantes' hand. In the case of *The Hospital of the Rotten (El hospital de los podridos)*, different theories surround its origins. Some critics credit it to Cervantes, who died in 1616, based on an attribution in a 1624 pamphlet that has since disappeared. The earliest known published version appears as an unattributed piece in a 1617 collection of comedias by Lope de Vega, one of Cervantes' great literary rivals. Nevertheless, in his 1878 *Guide to Spain and Portugal*, Henry George O'Shea mentions a letter by Cervantes attached to a copy of this play that he discovered in the University of Seville library. Dámaso Alonso in 1936 also attributes it to Cervantes, as does José Manuel Blecua in 1958. Blecua also attributes *The Chatterboxes (Los habladores)* to Cervantes.

The Election of the Mayors of Daganzo is included in Cervantes' 1615 collection, *Ocho comedias y ocho entremeses nuevos, nunca representados (Eight Comedies and Eight New Interludes, Never Before Performed)*. Unlike other Spanish Golden Age plays, and probably due to the mystery surrounding their authorship, neither *The Hospital of the Rotten* nor *The Chatterboxes* have received much attention from English literary translators. However, their language usage, word games, and conceptual twists provide for a challenging and fun translation. The plays' plots, characters, and humorous tone, among other characteristics, offer a timeless critique of the human condition. While *The Election of the Mayors of Daganzo* has been translated several times as part of the Cervantes volume, *The Chatterboxes* has rarely been translated and we have been unable to find a complete translation at all of *The Hospital of the Rotten*. We included *The Mayors* to show the similarities between the attributed Cervantes and the suspected.

Translation challenges

In translating these plays, we had to come to terms with the fact that usually the *entremés* is built upon quick verbal exchanges and sharp wit—sometimes, even at the expense of the plot. These three plays hold up a mirror that reflects the absurdities and frustrations inherent in some social behaviors and communication.

Some people argue that translators are the poor relations of a literary field which prizes either creative writers or literary critics. However, a good translator is, in fact, a skilled exponent of both disciplines. In order to do justice to the source material, the translator must have an understanding of historical, sociological, and literary contexts, before even beginning the "creative" writing required to capture the essence of the text. Otherwise, simply running the text through a Web translation program would be sufficient to produce artistic, poetic prose, instead of the garbled nonsense that usually results.

A skill for creative writing definitely comes into play when interpreting the lines. Simply using a literal translation will not work. The translator must have an awareness of both history and cultural traditions. In the case of a play, the translator must also be aware of how the work will "translate" to a physical space. These plays are translated to be performed—and through performance, to come to an understanding of Spanish Golden Age culture as well as the rich wordplay of the period. The translations are in modern English for a modern audience, but we have tried to retain the flavor of the time in which they were written. At some point, the translator has to accept that, if one is to adhere to a "strict" translation of a 17th-century text, there are things that the reader might not understand. It is then that we must trust the skills of the director or dramaturge. For the same reason, we have resisted the urge to add stage directions that were not in the original text. Spanish Golden Age *entremeses* were performed with minimal sets, leaving the text to drive the action.

Translation is all about questions and choices. Is it possible to translate a play without knowledge of the genre and without some background in theater? Do our cultural backgrounds affect our choices positively or negatively? While the translator's intention should be to stay outside the source material without interference, in reality, the finished piece is a collaboration between the original author and the translator. We must work with the author to convey the original intent.

A 'Rotten" translation: An example of process

To our knowledge this is the first complete translation of *The Hospital of the Rotten*. On its surface, it is a satire on contemporary medicine and bureaucracy. However, it is also a stinging critique of human foibles and social manias. The whole act takes place at the entrance of a new government-sponsored hospital, built specifically to remand those among the populace whose negative attitudes and petty complaints threaten to undermine the health of "proper" society—those considered rotten (*podridos*). Leiva is a visitor to whom the Director and the Secretary explain the hospital's purpose. The three men watch the arrival of a succession of potential patients, and comment on the validity of their maladies. Each new patient complains of an external irritant that causes them to decay and putrefy. The first *rotten* feels sorry for the subjects of an acquaintance who is appointed to be their governor, even though he wears "his slippers during the hottest part of the summer day" and carries his sword on the wrong side. A second rots about the influence of bad poets. While these malcontents are judged to be necessarily committed, a third man, who is consumed by jealousy at his neighbor's unending good fortune, is judged to have a valid complaint and is dismissed with official permission to, "Go with God and rot as much as you want." Other complaints include ugly men who are loved unjustly by beautiful women, people with big noses, people who eat with bibs, and doctors. There is also a couple who argue about her unfashionably-colored eyes and his too-large mouth.

Patients are prescribed a course of treatment—normally one that is as ridiculous as the original complaint. As the play progresses, Leiva, the Director and the Secretary become increasingly irritated and begin to exhibit the same behavior they have just diagnosed as rotten. Villaverde, the final candidate for hospitalization, turns the tables on the administrators and has them committed. Following the *entremés* tradition, the play ends with a song. Once all but Villaverde are locked up, he sings a comic song about people who rot and how he will not.

In this translation, the title itself led to many arguments and revisions. *Podridos* means rotten. However, in what sense is the word applied? In a hospital setting, there are wounds that rot. Food rots. Rotting can also be applied to a community in decay. In *El Hospital de los podridos*, rotten (*podridos*) also refers to the inner decay of the spirit, which leads one to complain and whine for little or no reason. This rotten spirit, in the minds of those who complain, manifests itself in physical decay. In this context, however, how does one find the perfect word that captures all of these meanings? *The Hospital of the Rottens* could be *A Hospital for Malcontents*, or *A Hospital of Complainers*. Possibly, *A Hospital of Complaints* would work if one recognizes that complaints can refer to both a physical and emotional condition. Ultimately, we decided to keep its most simple form —rotten. By doing so, we recognized all the possibilities inherent in the word and allow the reader to come to an understanding based on the events as they unfold.

Translation is an art that cannot be reproduced by a machine. For example, the Spanish "apenas puedo dar unas cintas a mi mujer' translates in an Internet translation as, "I can just give a few tapes to my wife," instead of, "I...can barely give my wife pretty ribbons." Some of the words used in the 17th century are defunct and as such are not even included in the program's database. For instance, the Secretary announces that one man rots "because there are so few discreet people, while there are many tailors and shoemakers." When asked what the complainant would prefer, the answer is "Albéitares y oficiales de jalmas asnátiles" which the Internet program translates as "Albéitares and jalmas asnátiles officers." Only the words "and" and "officers" are recognized. In order to determine what the phrase meant, we had to research old Spanish dictionaries for the out-of-favor words to determine that the phrase should be "Veterinarians and packers of donkey saddles." *Albéitares* is actually etymologically Arabic and has been replaced by the Spanish "veterinarios" in common usage. And of course, since donkeys are rarely the preferred mode of transportation nowadays, there is no room for people whose occupation is to pack their saddles, nor for a word that describes their trade.

A skill for creative writing definitely comes into play. Simply translating the words on the page will not work. For example, the lines, "que le echarán una melecina de esdrújulos de poetas, que le harán echar el ánima...," translate literally as, "That they will give him a medicine made of poets' verses that have the strength in the third to the last syllable that will make him throw out his soul." We decided to create a less-than-poetic phrase to capture the spirit of the piece, and translated it as, "...he will be given a medicine concocted from poor poets rotten rhymes that will make him vomit his soul." The alliterative wordplay in "poor poets rotten rhymes" reflects the "rotten rhymes" themselves, as the use of the word "esdrújulo" paired with "ánima" suggests in the original.

The translator must have an awareness of both history and cultural traditions. In the *entremés*, Leiva says that the rotten ones are increasing at such a rate that soon, "it will be necessary to have another New World for them to inhabit," obviously a reference to the Americas. It is a subtle jab at those who fled to the new continent. The implication is that the New World is already full of "rotten" people, so a "Newer World" is necessary to accommodate the increasing number of malcontents.

An awareness of historical context is necessary to allow the translator to appreciate and capture the nuances of the play. When the Secretary refers to the place running more accurately than a clock, it has the double meaning that the clocks of the time, while being advanced technology, could not be counted on for complete accuracy. Using the double-edged sword of dramatic irony, the author emphasizes the comedic unreliability of the Secretary's statements and the flaws in his judgment —ultimately, it is the Secretary who makes many of the decisions to commit the *podridos*.

Furthermore, in the *entremés*, an ambassador, who carries his sword in his left hand, is considered suspect by one of the *rotten*. A translator that is aware that the Latin *sinus* means "left," as well as being the etymological origin of the word *sinister*—and that in old tales, the left shoulder is where the devil sits, which leads to the superstition of throwing salt over the left shoulder—has an advantage when interpreting the author's satiric intention. The reference allows for the pun that if the official is left-handed, he cannot do things "right." Since this is said by a *rotten* who is about to be committed, it forces the reader to confront the ridiculousness of basing one's judgment on superstition and ignorance.

While there are few stage directions, some physical action may be necessary to understand the context of certain jokes. For example, the Secretary says a *podrido* rots, "because of doctors who, when one attempts to satisfy the bill, say, 'No, no. I do not want it,' but then hold their hand behind their back in the shape of a spoon." For the 17-century Spaniard, this pretense was probably a common occurrence. But nowadays, doctors are not paid directly so the reference may need to be explained, and the actor should make an obvious gesture of being paid behind the actor's back.

The playwright satirically recreates well-known situations in which the doctors use high-falutin' language and prescribe obviously ridiculous remedies. For instance, in *The Hospital of the Rotten,* the doctors take the pulse of those who complain of rotting due to malcontentment and state the following:

> This is bordering on satire! Let's put a stop to this by blocking his stomach with a plaster of tailor's apprentices, and fumigate him with ten hairs of the matchmaker Celestina's eyebrows, since from here I see more than four!

This is obviously a ridiculous diagnosis of the disease of satire, and an equally nonsensical prescription. A point of interest here is the reference to Celestina, a well-known literary character of the time. In our translation we chose to add the word "matchmaker" to aid our audience's understanding. We could have easily chosen to use the words "witch," "crone" or any number of other words to explain the cultural reference—a reference that would have required no explanation for a Spanish Golden Age audience.

The Hospital of the Rotten has a contemporary appeal. Although it was created at a time in which the government and the church tried to control medical advances, this interlude demonstrates a social concern. Therefore, it is possible to understand this play not only as a critique of, but also as a portrayal of, common concerns regarding new ways to heal. These attitudes can be transplanted to contemporary worries about psychological and social constructions. At the end of the play, those who make the decisions about who must be hospitalized start behaving like those whom they judge, resulting in their own commitment. Should we all be committed then? Are we all rotten?

A few more thoughts

The other two plays in this volume also raised interesting cultural and historical questions. For example, in *The Chatterboxes*, Roldán is a continuous talker who is equated with Sarmiento's wife, Beatriz. However, an in-depth reading leads us to observe that, in general, women were considered to be of a lesser social stature during that period. We know this because Roldán, who is clearly a rogue, represents a lower social class than Sarmiento, but suffers the same ailment as Beatriz. To continue with the gender stereotypification, it is implied in the text that Beatriz's condition afflicts all wives, but only a man can fix them. However, it should be noticed that, in the battle of wits, Beatriz and Roldán are truly equals.

Regarding *The Elections of the Mayors of Daganzo*, the characters bring historical baggage from 1492 when Jews and Muslims were expelled from the Iberian Peninsula—many renounced their faith and converted to Catholicism in order to remain in their homeland. During the last half of the 16th century, under the reign of Philip II of Spain, the Inquisition was still extremely active. This is why the councilmen are so concerned about presenting themselves as "old" Christians—not recently converted. In their dialogue, they constantly refer to saints and the divine and heaven to establish themselves as good Christians. For example, the character Pecan, which is a translation from *Algarrobo*—a word with Arabic roots—claims, "I am an old Christian, undoubtedly, and I believe in God completely." Clearly he is trying to convince the others of his moral credentials to choose a mayor and be an important part of society.

Each of the three plays is full of allusions to political and social conventions. The above mentioned are just a few examples. We leave it up to the readers and performers to discover the nuances of each play.

To conclude ...

Although these three plays were written more than 400 years ago, their themes still resonate. Reading and performing *The Hospital of the Rotten*, *The Chatterboxes* and *The Election of the Mayors of Dagazno* offers a chance to really explore the subtleties and intricacies of Spanish Golden Age texts and learn about turn-of-the-17th-century Spanish culture in a creative and fun way. Readers have a chance to explore the rich Golden Age culture with a depth that goes far beneath the apparent surface humor, and also to see that human nature has changed little. Despite the passage of four centuries, health care is still a hot-button issue, there is still way too much talking by people with little to say, and elections—well, not much has changed at all.

Catalina Castillón
Andy Coughlan

The Hospital of the Rotten
El hospital de los podridos

The Hospital of the Rotten is a hilarious satire on contemporary medicine and bureaucracy. However, it is also a stinging critique of human foibles and social manias. The action takes place at the entrance of a new government-sponsored hospital, built specifically to remand those "rotten" among the populace whose negative attitudes and petty complaints threaten to undermine the health of "proper" society. A succession of potential patients are judged on their various maladies, which become more and more ridiculous as the play progresses, with the prescribed treatments being equally ridiculous. Toward the end of the play, the hospital administrators become increasingly irritated and begin to exhibit the same behavior they have just diagnosed as rotten. The final candidate for hospitalization turns the tables on the administrators and has them committed. Following the *entremés* tradition, the play ends with a song.

A tip for the director
Historically, the characters should be played by the gender for which they were written. However, the translators believe that, with the exception of Villaverde and Clara, the characters may be played by males or females with pronoun adjustments.

Characters

LEIVA
DIRECTOR (Bald, glasses big nose)
PERO DÍAZ
SECRETARY (Officious)
DOCTOR
CAÑIZARES
MARISANTOS
TWO ORDERLIES (Big, bruising, bouncer types)
GÁLVEZ
CLARA
VILLAVERDE
VALENZUELA

Scene: The lobby of the hospital. White walls. Very antisceptic in feel.

Leiva, Director and Secretary enter

LEIVA (*crossing himself*)
Jesus! Jesus! Is it possible that such a hospital exists?

DIRECTOR
So much was rotten and putrid in this region that there was serious danger of an epidemic of disease, with more people dying because of it than die in a year of bubonic plague. So, in agreement with the

republic, according to the laws of good government, this hospital was founded so that those afflicted by this malady and pestilence may be cured. And I have been named director.

SECRETARY
After opening a ward for women, this town functions better than a well-oiled clock.

DIRECTOR
Let me tell you, Mr. Leiva. One man neither ate nor slept for hours on end. Instead, he heckled passersby. If he saw someone with a nice chain or a new dress he would say, "Who gave it to you, man? Where did you find it? Where did you get it? You do not own as much property as me, yet I, who have more than you, can barely give my wife pretty ribbons." He soon generated a poison or venom within him that caused him to faint. But let's just sit here and we will see the sick arrive.

The doctor enters taking the pulse of Cañizares

DOCTOR
Mr. Cañizares, I am afraid I cannot find anything wrong with you.

CAÑIZARES
How can that be? I have inside me a boiling rage and deep despair. It would be just my luck to find

out a tumor or abscess has overcooked inside my heart.

DOCTOR
What is it that has caused such putrefication?

CAÑIZARES
Just from one man. I despise him so much that if I even chance to see him on the street I must return home and I cannot go out again that day. I just curl up in a corner afraid that some horrible misfortune is going to befall me.

DOCTOR
Certainly, sir, there are those who seem to have a way about them that causes discomfort in others. For no reason, they are not generally well liked.

CAÑIZARES
Exactly so. How can you not expect me to rot and for a venomous gangrene to fester inside me when I see him wearing his slippers during the hottest part of the summer day, or to see that he carries his sword on the left?

DOCTOR
Why is it important to you that he wears his sword on the left or that he wears his slippers at midday?

CAÑIZARES
How could it not be important to me, in spite of
myself, if they are sending this man to be a governor
in one of the best places on earth?

DOCTOR
Ah, I see. You are rotting because you desire the
position yourself.

CAÑIZARES
What do you mean? I have never even considered it.
I rot because I think of those poor people who are to
be governed by this man. If he wears slippers at the
wrong time he will not be able to deal with business
quickly. And if he is a lefty, he will not be able to do
anything right.

DIRECTOR
Alright, Doctor. Place this rotten man in the hospital
and bring the others out.

DOCTOR (*leading Cañizares to the orderlies, who
are scoundrels*)
Come, brother, they will heal you in here.

*Cañizares is roughly dragged away. Doctor
follows.*

LEIVA
What a thing! That he should rot about it.

Pero Díaz and Marisantos enter.

PERO DÍAZ
Alright, leave me alone, Marisantos. I have not been able to drink, eat nor sleep since hearing such a thing.

MARISANTOS
But Pero Díaz, how can a man like you with your intelligence rot in such a way as to lose your appetite and take on such sorrow?

PERO DÍAZ
How can I not, knowing that there is a poet who writes such verse?
(*Theatrically*)   Playing, they were playing,
              Even chess, one day,
              The famous Spanish Emperor
              And the Moorish king of Almeria.
(*pronounce Almeri-ay for bad rhyme*)

MARISANTOS
What does it matter to you who wrote that?

PERO DÍAZ
It matters a lot! Because it is a slander against the Emperor. A prince of such majesty and irascibility would never sit down to play chess, a game of such impeturbabilty, even with the Moorish king of Almeri-ya. If this poet is still alive, I must make him

retract; and if he is dead, then I must see if he left a retraction in his last will and testament.

MARISANTOS
What pretty nonsense. You cannot eat or sleep because of that? What a foolish affliction you have taken.

DIRECTOR
Come here, brother. What is the cause of your rotting?

PERO DÍAZ (*Pause*)
The poets.

DIRECTOR
You are rotting inside because of the poets. What a hard time you are having. And which poets cause your distress?

PERO DÍAZ
Those who write Carols on Christmas nights that mix a thousand stupid remarks with heresy. You see, my lord, I gave one of them an octave by Garcilaso that says:
> Near the Tajo River, in pleasant solitude,
> Of green willows there is a thicket

He changed it to this:

> Near God, in pleasant solitude,
> Of green *saints* there is a thicket

And when someone asked who these saints were, the poet said they were St. Phillip and St. James, and other saints celebrated during the *spring*!

DIRECTOR
That certainly is some silly nonsense.

PERO DÍAZ
One Christmas night I went inside a local church and I heard a choir singing:

> When Jesus comes out to his corridors,
> Beelzebub does not appear, and Satan hides

And when I asked whose song it was, one answered, "Mine," very satisfied, as if he had done a great thing. And another was also singing this:

> What do you do in this manger,
> My Lord, because of the ungrateful man?
> Shoo a cat, shoo a cat!

DIRECTOR
Do not wonder; because those poets are as wintery as melons.

PERO DÍAZ
My insides also rot with those poets who think they

know, but do not know—and with others who know, but do not think.

DIRECTOR
Explain yourself. What does that mean; "They know, but do not think?"

PERO DÍAZ
That there are poets who know what they do, and because they do not think well, they condemn us all to hell.

DIRECTOR
This man is in urgent need of a remedy. It would be a good idea to deliver him to the company of bad poets so that they may cure him.

PERO DÍAZ
No! For the love of God ...

DIRECTOR (*beckoning to the orderlies*)
Oh, orderlies. Take this rotten one away.

They drag a struggling and protesting Pero Díaz away.

LEIVA
Surely, there is no rotting worse than his.

DIRECTOR
We shall see. Here comes another one. You will learn more from him.

Valenzuela enters, talking to himself.

VALENZUELA
How can there be such a thing? That a man is so lucky that whatever he turns his hands to is a success? And here am I, with poison festering throughout my body and pus oozing out from every pore.

DIRECTOR (*to the Secretary*)
From what is this man suffering?

SECRETARY
Sir, he is furious and rotting from his anger. This man is afflicted by his neighbor, whose every undertaking is a roaring success.

DIRECTOR
I see he is in bad shape, but surely that is more a case of envy than putrefication?

VALENZUELA
What do you mean envy? Let the Devil take me if that is all it is, Mr. Director. Such a stingy and greedy man should not enjoy success.

DIRECTOR
You are right; these types do not deserve their luck.
(*To Leiva*) If anyone has good reason to rot, it is he.
(*To Valenzuela*) You will be given leave to rot for
three days a week.

VALENZUELA
What do you mean, three days? I shall rot more for
not rotting.

DIRECTOR
As you wish. Go with God and rot as much as you
want.

VALENZUELA
Gracias. I kiss your hand in gratitude for such favor.

Valenzuela leaves, and GÁLVEZ comes out.

GÁLVEZ
To think of a woman with such bad taste! She is
probably why they say, "There are eyes that fall in
love with 'sleep boogers!'"

DIRECTOR
About what is this brother complaining?

SECRETARY
He is disgusted because a very beautiful woman
from this town is in love with a bald man who wears
glasses.

DIRECTOR
So? You rot because of that, my good man? What is
it to you if she has bad taste in men?

GÁLVEZ
How is it not important to me? I would prefer to see
her love a demon. How can such a beauty love a
bespectacled-baldy man?

DIRECTOR (*to Lieva*)
See how infuriated he is about this?

GÁLVEZ
How can I not rage about this? Tell me sir, what sort
of woman could wake up and see a bald man by her
side, looking like a skull or a pumpkin, because that
is how a bald man looks? Or how can she look
lovingly into his eyes, knowing they are so bad?

DIRECTOR
That it. You are rotten. Orderlies, put this rotten one
away.

GÁLVEZ
Me sir? Why? (*He is dragged away*)

LEIVA
The rotten ones are decaying and are spreading ruin. If we do not remedy this situation, they will multiply in such numbers that it will be necessary to have another New World for them to inhabit.

DIRECTOR
Please read that list, Mr. Secretary.

Secretary takes out some papers and reads them.

SECRETARY
There is a man here who rots about those who have big noses.

DIRECTOR
The Devil take him! What is it to him whether people have big or small noses?

SECRETARY
He says that every day one of the big-nosed fellows walks down his narrow street, and that when he does it is necessary to walk sideways in order to pass him by. And besides that inconvenience, he says there is another whose nose is so big that his handkerchiefs could double as boat sails.

DIRECTOR (*blowing his nose*)
That man has a rotten humor.

SECRETARY
There is another man who rots because some people
eat wearing bibs.

DIRECTOR
In this case, he may be on the right path. Such
people look like they are ebony guitars with white
panels—and they look like women. However, notify
this man he has three days to recover from this
rotten state. If not, he will be given a medicine
concocted from poor poet's rotten rhymes that will
make him vomit his soul—an ointment prepared
from the brains of said poets.

SECRETARY (*Thoughtfully to himself*)
Are there enough poet's brains throughout the world
to fill even half a hazelnut shell? How much more
than that would be needed? It would take at least
four ounces of the stuff to complete the pharmacist's
art.

DIRECTOR
Read on!

SECRETARY
Here is another who rots because of doctors who,
when one attempts to satisfy the bill, says, "No, no. I
do not want it," but then hold their hand behind
their back in the shape of a spoon.

DIRECTOR
Ah, that one has good reason to complain. Why do
they make such affectations when they would take
even more if we were willing to give it?

SECRETARY
Another rots because there are so few discreet
people, while there are many tailors and
shoemakers.

DIRECTOR
So? What would he have instead?

SECRETARY
Veterinarians and packers of donkey saddles.

DIRECTOR
This is bordering on satire! Let's put a stop to this by
blocking his stomach with a plaster of tailor's
apprentices, and fumigate him with ten hairs of the
matchmaker Celestina's eyebrows, since from here I
see more than four!

*Secretary pauses, shakes head as if confused,
writes in notebook.*

SECRETARY
Here there are some old ladies who are rotting
because their neighbors hens lay bigger eggs and
have better chickens.

DIRECTOR
They are trivial complaints. Just toss these old ladies some powder of straw figs.

SECRETARY
There is also a married couple. The husband is rotting because the wife has blue eyes and the wife is rotting because the husband's mouth is too big.

DIRECTOR
They might be reasonable people. Bid them come out here. I want to meet them

CLARA and VILLAVERDE come out arguing with each other.

CLARA
Pish, my lord; it will be much better if you rot from seeing your deformed mouth, that looks like the mouth of an oven, and let me be with my eyes, blue or green.

DIRECTOR (*Softly*)
Come here, brother. You rot because of that? Because your wife has blue eyes?

VILLAVERDE
Yes, sir. Blue eyes are no longer fashionable. The trend now is for black eyes.

DIRECTOR
What foolishness. If God gave her eyes like that, what is she expected to do?

VILLAVERDE
She should use her skills to dye them. It is due to our constant fighting that my mouth split wide open.

DIRECTOR
What utter nonsense. I have never seen anything like it in my life. Therefore, it is necessary to prescribe you fire buds that burn with the errors of doctors and apothecaries

VILLAVERDE
Those are even worse than the mistakes of the lawyers. Their mistakes will only cost you your purse, but doctors' mistakes will cost you your health—or your life!

LEIVA
Mr. Secretary, this lady is the wife of this man?

SECRETARY
Don't you see it my lord?

LEIVA (*Drops to his knees*)
Jesus! Jesus! Jesus, a thousand times, Jesus!

SECRETARY
Why are you crossing yourself?

LEIVA
Shouldn't I cross myself, when such a beautiful lady
is married to such an ugly man as this one, who
looks like a beetle?

SECRETARY (*Slyly*)
So you are rotting because of this, my lord?

LEIVA
Well, How can you not expect me to rot and become
venomous inside at seeing such a thing? This lady
deserves a prince for a husband, and he should be
an angel in appearance and in bearing.

SECRETARY (*aside*)
He is a raving lunatic! Orderlies! Put this rotten one
inside!

LEIVA
Me? Why?
Leiva is dragged away.

DIRECTOR
Mister secretary, have you ever seen a man of such
good intelligence go crazy in such a way?

SECRETARY
Does that give you pain and sorrow?

DIRECTOR
Well, shouldn't it upset me, in spite of myself, to see
that a man that I thought had a great reputation,
and was very sane and prudent, has lost his sanity?

SECRETARY
You are rotten my lord. (*Beckons menacingly with
his finger*) Oh, Orderlies!

DIRECTOR
Me? Mr. Secretary!

Director is dragged away.

CLARA
Mr. Secretary, I am really amazed that a man like
your lordship did not have a better ending with Mr.
Director.

SECRETARY
So, you rot because of that, my lady?

CLARA
Well, Shouldn't I rot, seeing the obligation that your
lordship has to him, he being superior in everything,
not to respect Mr. Director better? One has just to
see his authority and not treat him the way your
lordship did ...

SECRETARY
Listen, listen, how lost is this sister, how lost she is!
Oh, orderlies, take this sister to the ward.

CLARA
Me, my lord? See here sir ...

Clara is dragged away.

SECRETARY
Mr. Villaverde, is that lady your wife?

VILLAVERDE
She is my wife. Why do you ask, sir?

SECRETARIO
I ask because you see her being taken away and yet
you remain so calm.

VILLAVERDE
Why shouldn't I be?

SECRETARY
Good grief. Do not tell me that or you will make me
hurl these papers and lose my patience with you. A
man like your lordship, one who seems so
honorable. Don't you have the obligation to feel
sorry for your wife's misfortune?

VILLAVERDE (*aside*)
This man is rotten. (*To Secretary)* You will not
escape from the hospital. (*In the same tone as
Secretary has previously used*) Oh, orderlies!

*Secretary is dragged away. Villaverde gets a
guitar and sings.*

> Nobody should rot
> about what others do.
>
> Since all of your life
> Plays like a game of poker
> Where everything is a gamble
> And the best just do it better;
>
> Let people live under
> The laws they prefer
> Though we may judge their lives
> To be an uproar.
>
> The one who boasts of cleaning
> The Muses' chamber pots,
> Can actually be the companion
> Of those who graze in the forts.
>
> Smart is he, who being used
> To eating special treats
> Is never found without a hen
> To at least have eggs to eat.

And with the power of rouge
Of corrosive mercury and white lead
The woman who is a devil in figure
Seeks to be angelic instead.

See in what manner they go
Those who are eaten by sorrows
And angered and saddened
By other people's foibles.

Nobody should rot
about what others do.

Take me, for example,
If in the street I see
Two men fighting with knives
I lock my sword with a key;

And since I look through spectacles,
If the arrogant astrologer
Lies in his repertoire,
I try to shy away from anger.

If the sun comes out at midday
And I put on brand new shoes
If it should rain I will gladly bear
Such a horrible misfortune;

And if the tailor should steal my cloth,
So that my suit does not come out right,

Fitting me either too loose
Or else fitting me too tight;

And if you like this comedy,
Or if you say it's nonsense;
If the people come or not come,
If they talk or listen in silence,

Even though they think me odd
Or think me a cold fish,
I have no intention to rot,
Nor to end my happiness.

End.

The Chatterboxes
Los Habladores

Doña Beatriz: ¿Cómo exquisito? Mal sabe vuesa merced de exquisitos: toda cosa exquisita es extraordinaria; la ordinaria no causa admiración; ... de cosas ... alta cosa d... do es ... e ... di... ... es ... en to... ... ...ento ...ón.

... dij... ...rced, ...rque... ...res ...os s... ...n; ...e l... ...este ...e, y los casados son o... ...os a quererse, amarse y estimarse...

A surface reading would suggest that this play is a satire on the talkative wife who needs to be tamed. However, since the main chatterbox is male, the play takes this stereotype and twists it. The action begins on the street where Sarmiento meets Roldán, a *pícaro*, a rogue who makes his way by talking incessantly without making any sense. Sarmiento hires him to "cure" his wife who suffers from the same affliction—incessant chatter. He is convinced that Roldán will be able to talk her into silence. The action shifts to Sarmiento's house, where a battle of wits—or at least a battle of tongues—ensues. When the police arrive to arrest Roldán, the play twists again. Exactly who has the upper hand? As usual, it ends in a song.

A Tip for the Director

The incessant chatting should almost be rythmical and the actors should make full use of their physicality to emphasize the nonsensical dialogue. Preferably, the characters of Roldán and Sarmiento should be male and Beatriz should be female. The other characters can be male or female with script adjustments. Most of the stage directions in this play are original, with some additions by the translators for contextual interpretation.

Characters

ROLDÁN
SARMIENTO
DOÑA BEATRIZ (Sarmiento's wife)
INÉS (a maid)
SOLICITOR
BAILIFF
SECRETARY
POLICEMAN

(*Enter the solicitor and Sarmiento, who has his hat in his hand. Behind them comes Roldán in a ragged habit, leather vest, a sword — and socks*)

SARMIENTO
Take the 200 ducets, Mr. Solicitor, and upon my word, sir, even if it had cost me 400, it would still be pleasing because the wound would have required double the stitches.

SOLICITOR
Your worship has acted as a gentleman in giving it, and as a Christian, in paying it. And I take the money, happy that it will ease me and it will remedy him.

ROLDÁN
Ah gentleman, is your worship a solicitor?

SOLICITOR
Yes I am. What do you command, sir?

ROLDÁN
What money is that?

SOLICITOR
This gentleman gives it to me to pay the man upon whom he inflicted a wound requiring 12 stitches.

ROLDÁN
And how much is the money?

SOLICITOR
200 ducets.

ROLDÁN
Go with God, your worship.

SOLICITOR
God keep you, your worship.

(*Solicitor exits*)

ROLDÁN
Ah, sir.

SARMIENTO
Me, my good man?

ROLDÁN
To your worship, I talk.

SARMIENTO
What do you want?

ROLDÁN
Cover yourself, sir, otherwise I will not say a word.

(*Sarmiento puts on his hat*)

SARMIENTO
I am covered.

ROLDÁN
My lord, I am a poor nobleman, although I have a good reputation. I have a need, and I have learned that your worship has given 200 ducets to a man whom you have stabbed once. If your worship takes pleasure in stabbing people, I come here so your worship can give me one, wherever is your pleasure, and I will take it for 50 ducets less than the other.

SARMIENTO
If I was not crestfallen, you would make me laugh, your lordship—are you serious? Come here. Don't you think stabbings should be given only to those who deserve it?

ROLDÁN
Who deserves them more than necessity? Don't they
say necessity has the face of a heretic. And who
deserves a facial scar more than a heretic?

SARMIENTO
Your worship must not be very well read. The Latin
proverb says, "*necessitas caret lege,*" which mean,
"necessity lacks law."

ROLDÁN
Your worship speaks very well. Because the law was
invented for peace, and reason is the soul of the law.
And whoever has a soul has the potencies. There are
three potencies of the soul: memory, will and
understanding. Your worship has very good
understanding. The understanding is known in the
physiognomy—and your worship's physiognomy is
perverse for the concurrence of Saturn and Jupiter.
Even though Venus sees you in the quarter of the
tenth ascendant sign of the horoscope.

SARMIENTO
By the devil that brought me here, this is just what I
need after having paid 200 ducets for a stabbing.

ROLDÁN
Stabbing, did you say, your worship? That is well
said. A stabbing is what Cain gave his brother Abel,
even though the knives did not then exist. A

stabbing? That's what Alexander the Great gave to Queen Pantasilea, after taking Zamora away from her, the well-protected city. And also Julius Cesar to Don Pedro Anzures, about playing chess with Don Gaiferos, between Cabañas and Olias. But be warned, your worship, that wounds can be given in two ways. There is treason and premeditation: Treason is committed against the king, and premeditation is committed against one's equals. By the arms they should be, and if I would fight with advantage, because Caranza in his "Philosophy of the Sword" and Terence in "Conjuring of Catirina …"

SARMIENTO
The devil take you, you are driving me crazy. Don't you see that what you say is not true—it's nonsense?

ROLDÁN
Nonsense, says your worship? You say it very well. Like a nun, like Bernadina, which is a very pretty name. A woman whose name is Bernardina should become a nun of the order of St. Bernard, because if her name was Francisca that couldn't be because the Franciscas have four Fs, and the F is one of the letters of the ABC. The letters of the ABC are 23. The K is used in Castillian when we are children, because it is then when we say "caca," which is twice that sound of the letter K. Two times can be of wine— the wine has many virtues. It cannot be taken when fasting, nor when too watery because the rare parts

of the water penetrate the pores and go up to the brain and enters pure ...

SARMIENTO
Hold on! You are killing me! I think that some devil has got hold of your tongue.

ROLDÁN
Your worship says it very well, because whoever has a tongue goes to Rome ... . I have been in Rome and in La Mancha, in Transylvania and in Puebla de Montalvan. Montalvan was a castle from where the lord Reynaldos hailed. Reynaldo was one of the twelve pairs of friends, one of those who ate with the Emperor Charlemagne at the Round Table. In Valladolid there is a little square called el Ochavo—like the coin that is worth half a quarter. A quarter is compounded of four maravedis. The old maravedi was worth as much as an escudo is worth now. There are two types of those coins; there are shields of patience and shields of ...

SARMIENTO
May god give me patience to suffer you! Hold on, you are going to get me lost!

ROLDÁN
Lost, said your worship, and said it very well, because losing is not winning, and there are seven ways to lose; to lose at gambling, to lose one's

65

possessions, to lose friends, to lose one's honor, to lose one's sanity, to lose one's ring or handkerchief though carelessness, to lose …

SARMIENTO
Enough, by the devil!

ROLDÁN
The devil, said your worship, and said it very well, because the devil tempts us with various temptations. The biggest of them all is the flesh— the flesh is like meat and not fish. The fish is phlegmish. The phlegmatic are not choleric. Man is composed of four elements; anger, blood, phlegm and melancholy. Melancholy is not happiness, because happiness consists of having money. Money makes the man. Men are not beasts, beasts graze; and finally …

SARMIENTO
And finally, your worship will drive me mad! I beg you, as a courtesy, let me get a word in—without telling me what a word is! Or I will fall down dead!

ROLDÁN
What does your worship command?

SARMIENTO
My lord, I have a wife who, by my sins, is the greatest chatterbox the world has ever seen since

there have been women in this world. She talks in such a manner that I have caught myself, many times, thinking of killing her because of her words, as others do because of actions. I have searched for remedies, none of which have been appropriate. It seems to me that if I take your worship to my house and you speak with her for six days without interruption, you will change her in the manner of those who start being valiant in front of those who have been valiant for many days. Come with me, your worship, I beg you. I want to pretend that your worship is my cousin. Under this pretext, I will have you in my house.

ROLDÁN
Cousin, your worship said, and said it very well. We call first cousin our father's brother's son. First, as the shoemaker works for the first time. First, as one of the strings on a guitar. The guitar is composed of five orders. There are only four orders of mendicant monks. Four is not five. But against five, in the old times, one who challenged the common was required to fight against five—as it was seen in Don Diego Ordoñez and the sons of Arias Gonzalo, when the King Don Sancho ...

SARMIENTO
Hold on! Be quiet, by God! Come with me and you will say the rest over there.

ROLDÁN
Lead the way, your worship, and in two hours I will turn that woman mute as a stone, because the stone ...

SARMIENTO
I will not hear another word!

ROLDÁN
Then walk, that I will heal your wife.

(*Exit Sarmiento and Roldán. Action shifts to Sarmiento's house. Doña Beatriz and Inés, her maid, enter*)

BEATRIZ
Inís! Hello Inís! What do I say? Inís, Inís.

INÉS
I hear you, my lady my lady, my lady.

BEATRIZ
Rogue, shameless. How dare you respond to me with that language. Don't you know that shame is the principal jewel of women.

INÉS
My lady, just to talk, even when you have nothing to say, you call me 200 times.

BEATRIZ
You rascal! The number 200 is a big number under
which you can understand 200 thousand by adding
zeros. The zeros do not have any value in them
selves ...

INÉS
My lady, I understand! Tell me what I must do, or
we will waste our time chatting.

BEATRIZ
Do not waste time. You have to set the table for our
lord to eat. You know that he has been crestfallen for
a while, and crestfallen, in a married man, is cause
for him to raise a stick, and starting with the maids,
finishes with the lady.

INÉS
Then, if there is no more than setting the table, I will
fly and do it.

(*Inís exits. Sarmiento and Roldán arrive*)

SARMIENTO
Hello? Anybody home? Doña Beatriz. Hello?

BEATRIZ
Here I am, my lord. Why are you shouting?

SARMIENTO
Look, I bring this gentleman, a soldier and relative of mine, as a guest. Take care of him and dote on him, because he is aspiring to the court.

BEATRIZ
If your worship goes to the court, you should be warned that the court, is not for a timid Carlos, because timidity is the lineage of the foolish, and the fool is close to being destitute and he deserves it, because understanding is the light of human actions, and every action consists ...

ROLDÁN
Slowly, slowly, I beg your ladyship. I know well that it consists on the disposition of nature, because nature works on the corporeal instruments and disposes the senses. And the senses are five; to walk, to touch, to run and to think, and not to obstruct. Every person who obstructs is ignorant, and ignorance consists of not falling on things. He who falls and gets up, God gives him high holidays. High holidays are four—Christmas, Three Kings, Easter and Pentecost. Pentecost is an exquisite term ...

BEATRIZ
How come exquisite? Your worship knows little about exquisites. Every exquisite thing is extraordinary—the ordinary does not inspire admiration. Admiration is born of high things. The

highest thing in the world is quietude, because nobody reaches it. The lowest thing is malice, because everybody falls in it. Falling is inevitable, because there are three states in everything; beginning, augmenting and declining.

ROLDÁN
Declining, your ladyship said, and you said it very well. Because in grammar, names decline, verbs are conjugated, and those who get married are called by that name. And those who are conjugal are obligated to love, appreciate and esteem each other as commanded by the holy mother church. And the reason for this is ...

BEATRIZ
Wait, wait! What is this, husband? Have you lost your mind? What man is this that you have brought to my house?

SARMIENTO (*aside*)
By God, I am happy. I have my payback, now.

(*to Beatriz*)

Set the table quickly that we may eat. Mr. Roldán will be my guest for six or seven years.

BEATRIZ
Seven years! Bad years! Not even an hour, my

husband, or I will burst.

SARMIENTO
He would have made a good husband for you. Hello!
Bring the food.

(*Inés enters*)

INÉS
We have guests? Here is the table.

ROLDÁN
Who is this lady?

SARMIENTO
It is the maid of the house.

ROLDÁN
A maid in Valencia is called *fadrina*; in Italy,
masara; in France, *gaspirria;* in Germany,
filimoquia; in the court, *servant*; in the Basque
country, *moscorra*; and among rogues, *daifa*. Bring
the food merrily, I want your worships to see me eat
as they do in Great Britain.

BEATRIZ
There is nothing to do here but lose our minds.
Husband, I am bursting to speak.

ROLDÁN
To speak, your ladyship said, and you said it well. It is through speaking that concepts are understood. These concepts are formed in the understanding. He who does not understand does not feel. He who does not feel does not live. He who does not live is dead. He who is dead must be thrown in the vegetable patch.

BEATRIZ
Husband! Husband!

SARMIENTO
What is it, woman?

BEATRIZ
Throw this man out of here with the devil. I am bursting to speak.

SARMIENTO
Woman, be patient. He cannot leave from here until seven years have passed. I have given my word and I am obligated to keep it, or I would not be who I am.

BEATRIZ
Seven years! I will die before that. Ay! Ay! Ay!

(*She falls dramatically*)

INÉS
She fainted. Is this what my lord wants to see before

your eyes? To see her there—dead?

ROLDÁN
God almighty! What has caused this malady? Not
speaking?

(*There's a knocking at the door. There's a voice
from outside*)

BAILIFF
Open up for the justice, open up for the justice!

ROLDÁN
The justice? Oh, poor me. I am on the run and if
they recognize me they will take me to jail.

SARMIENTO
Well, sir, the solution is to get inside this rug that
has been readied for cleaning. Then you can be safe.
I cannot see another way.

(*Roldán hides inside a rug that is folded over a line.
Bailiff, Secretary and Policeman enter*)

BAILIFF
About time you opened the door.

SARMIENTO
What is it that your worship wants that you are so
furious?

BAILIFF
The Governor commands, even though your worship
has already paid the 200 ducets for the stabbing,
that you come to shake hands with the man, and to
embrace and to be friends.

SARMIENTO
I would like to eat first.

SECRETARY
The man is nearby, and then your worship may
return and eat at your leisure.

SARMIENTO
Let's go. Meanwhile, set the table.

(*Sarmiento, Bailiff, Secretary and Policeman leave*)

INÉS
Wake up, my lady. If you fainted for not speaking,
now you are alone and you may speak whenever you
please.

BEATRIZ
Thanks to the lord. Now I will rest from the silence I
had before.

(*Roldán sticks his head out of the rug*)

ROLDÁN
Silence, your ladyship said, and you said it very well, because silence was always praised by the wise men. And wise men sometimes remain quiet and sometimes speak. Because there are times for speaking and there are times for silence. Whoever is silent consents, and consent is given in writing, and a legal document needs three witnesses. And if it is a sealed testament, seven witnesses, because …

BEATRIZ
Because, let the devil take you! You and whomever brought you here. Such wickedness! I faint—again.

(*She half faints into a chair. Roldán ducks back behind the rug as Sarmiento, Bailiff, Secretary and Policeman enter*)

SARMIENTO
Since friendships have been made, I would like your worships to share a drink. Hello! Bring me a bottle and that pear liqueur.

(*Beatriz rises and takes a carpet beater from next to the rug*)

BEATRIZ
Now you get us into this? Don't you see we are busy beating these rugs?

(*She shows the beater to Inés*)

You take that other one and let's beat this rug until it is clean.

(*Roldán jumps out*)

ROLDÁN
Wait, wait, my ladies. I well understood that you spoke a lot, but not that you played by hand.

BAILIFF
Listen! What is this? Isn't this that rogue Roldanejo, the chatterbox? The conman?

SECRETARY
One and the same.

BAILIFF
Consider yourself under arrest.

ROLDÁN
Arrested, said your lordship, and you said it very well, because the arrested is not free, and freedom ...

BAILIFF
No! No! No! Your chattering has no effect here. As god lives, you are going to jail.

SARMIENTO
Mr. Bailiff. I beg your worship, that since he was
found in my house, this time he is not taken. I give
you my word that I will give him whatever he needs
to leave this place once he has cured my wife.

BAILIFF
Cured of what?

SARMIENTO
Of talking.

BAILIFF
How?

SARMIENTO
By talking. Because he talks so much, he mutes her.

BAILIFF
I am fine with that so I can see that miracle. But it
must be with the condition that if he cures her, your
worship tells me right away, so that I may take him
to my house. My wife has the same infirmity, and it
would make me happy if he cured her, also.

SARMIENTO
I will inform you whatever happens.

ROLDÁN
I know I will leave her well cured.

BAILIFF
Go, chatterbox, go.

SARMIENTO
These words do not displease me.

BAILIFF
If you like those words, listen. I have some poetry.

ROLDÁN
Listen! Poetry, said your worship, then pay
attention. By god, the poetic duel begins.

(*They all bow to each other and they take turns
speaking*)

BAILIFF
The condition of talking
Seems to be a temptation
For those who usually tempt us;
And can be a condition
Of men from the dungheap.
He beats like a drummer
With that tongue, the conman;
Whose words, with loud noise,
Ring in discreet ears.

Go, chatterbox, go.

(*Bailiff bows to Secretary*)

SECRETARY
After death, I know
They will write his epitaph,
Saying, "Here lies one
Who will not be quiet in death
As much as he spoke alive."

INÉS
I want to finish that line

SECRETARY
Go ahead, let's hear.

INÉS
And since the rigor of talking
To a dead man gives fear,
Go to a mountain, where no one
Will be bothered by your talk,

Go, chatterbox, go.

(*She bows to Sarmiento*)

SARMIENTO
Here goes my line.

Oh you, who spoke for twenty,
And spoke for twenty thousand ...

BEATRIZ
Stop! I will finish it.

ROLDÁN
By talking—you are not subtle.

BEATRIZ
Pay attention, mister relative.

Go to where your rumour
Will not discredit you,
And, since your talent is known
Go, sick of the tongue,

Go, chatterbox, go.

(*She bows to Roldán*)

ROLDÁN
Listen, and pay attention, your worships,
My line will not be worse.

I came to cure a chatterbox
Who never stopped her patter.
And I plan, from now on,
To mute her with my chatter.
This gentleman invited me,
And I will eat, although,
To avoid feeding me, his wife says ...

Go, chatterbox, go.
(*All exit, bowing to each other*)

End.

The Election of the Mayors of Daganzo
La elección de los alcaldes de Daganzo

By Miguel de Cervantes Saavedra

This wonderful satire on governmental aptitudes takes in the village of Daganzo, where the city councilors are meeting to elect the next mayor. They decide to test each of the prospective candidates. When the four applicants arrive, each boasts about a peculiar quality which they believe makes them uniquely qualified for the position. Both the candidates and the councilors have very interesting ideas on what makes a perfect city leader. The entrance of an old priest and a band of gypsies add to the insanity of this hilarious electoral process. Who would earn your vote? The play ends with a song.

A Tip for the Director

The names were translated from the original and offer some insight into the characters' personalities. The candidates' physicality may reflect the names. All characters, with the exception of the gypsy girl indicated in the song, may be played by males or females with script adjustments as necessary.

Characters

The City Council:
HOOF, an academic
PETER SNEEZE, the council secretary
CRUMB, a councilman
ALONSO PECAN, a councilman

The mayoral candidates:
JOHN ROCK
FRANCIS SMOKE
MICHAEL HAMHOCK
PETER FROG

Others:
UNO, a servant (One, anybody)
FRIAR, an old priest
GYPSIES (male and female)

(*Crumb, Sneeze, Hoof and Pecan enter, talking among themselves*)

CRUMB
At ease, everything will come out alright
If the blessed heavens so wish.

PECAN
Let's roll the dice and not sell it.

CRUMB
Peace, it will be easy to get out of this business well, heaven willing.

PECAN
Heaven willing or not, it is important.

CRUMB
Pecan, your tongue is slipping. Speak cautiously and to the point, your words do not sound good to me. "Heaven willing or not," by Saint Junco! You boast that you know it all and you rush into everything without thinking.

PECAN
I am an old Christian, undoubtedly, and I believe in God completely.

HOOF
Good, we shouldn't want for anything more.

PECAN
If by chance, I misspoke, I confess I am a goose! I take back what I said.

SNEEZE
Enough! God wants nothing more from the worst sinner than to live and repent.

PECAN
I say that I live and repent, and I know that heaven can do whatever it wishes,
Without anybody being able to control its hand—especially when it rains.

CRUMB
From the clouds, Pecan, the water comes from the clouds, not from heaven.

PECAN
Body of the world, if we come here to reproach each other, let it be said.
In faith, Pecan is worthy of reproach at every step.

HOOF
Redeamus ad rem—Let's get back to the topic, Mr. Crumb and Mr. Pecan. Let's not waste our time with childish excuses. Are we all together here for impertinent disputes?
(*Aside*) What a thing. Every time Crumb and Pecan get together there arises a thousand thunderstorms of a thousand contradictory intentions among them.

SNEEZE
Professor Hoof is right. Let's get back to the point. Let's see which mayoral candidates we will nominate for next year, that are such that cannot be rejected in the capital, Toledo, but will be approved —this is the reason for our meeting.

CRUMB
There are four suitors for the mace—John Rock,
Francis Smoke, Michael Hamhock and Peter Frog.
These are all men of prudence and good judgment
that could govern not only Daganzo, but even Rome.

PECAN
And little Roman.

SNEEZE
Anything else to point out? (*Aside*) By St. Pito, let
me out of this group.

PECAN
It seems appropriate that the scribe's name is
Sneeze, because the smoke builds up in him. (*to
Sneeze*) Calm down, I will say nothing.

CRUMB
There must be found, perchance, in all the oval ...

PECAN
What do you mean oval? Like eggs? You suck eggs?
My dear Crumb, say "globe" and it will be good for
you.

CRUMB
What I am trying to say is that, in the entire world, it
is not possible to find four geniuses better than
these candidates.

PECAN
At least I know that Rock has the most beautiful
distinction ...

SNEEZE
For what?

PECAN
... to be divine for heaps of property and a taste for
wines. In my house, a few days ago, he tasted a
barrel and he said that the clear wine tasted like a
stick, like leather and like iron. When the barrel was
finished, we found at the bottom a twig, and from
that twig hung a belt and a small key.

SNEEZE
Oh what a rare skill, what a rare ability. He will
govern well, the person who knows the difference
between Sherry, Roija and Bordeaux.

PECAN
Michael Hamhock is an eagle.

HOOF
In what way?

PECAN
He lugs his bow with a great arc.

HOOF
Is he that good a shot?

PECAN
So much so, that if it wasn't for the fact that with
most of his shots he twists his left hand, there would
not be a bird left in the whole region.

HOOF
That is a rare and necessary skill for a mayor to
have.

PECAN
What can I say about Francis Smoke? He darns
shoes as good as any tailor. Then Peter Frog? There
is not a memory that is his equal. He remembers
every line, without missing a letter, about the old
and famous dog of Alba.

CRUMB
He has my vote!

SNEEZE
And even mine.

PECAN
I stick with Rock.

HOOF
I don't vote for anybody unless they give us more
proof of their talent regarding jurisprudence.

PECAN
I have a good solution. Let's make the four
candidates come here so Mr. academic Hoof may
examine them. He knows about art and, according
to his science, we will see who should be nominated
for the position.

SNEEZE
Long life to God! That is a very rare admonition.

CRUMB (*He uses wrong words through ignorance,
and transposes letters*)
Advice that could have served to arbitrate for his
jamesty. Because in the court, there are rapamedics
—there could be rapamayors.

PECAN
"Para," Mr. Crumb, not "rapa."

CRUMB
There is no "dujge" like you in the whole world.

HOOF
Judge! In spite of all my sorrows.

SNEEZE
My god, this Pecan is impertinent.

PECAN
What I say is, since there are exams for the barbers,
the blacksmiths and the tailors, and also the
surgeons and other silly things, there should also be
a test for mayors—and the one that is found to be
sufficient and capable for that job, should be given a
diploma, which will prove his worth. He could put
the diploma in a white frame, and he could go to any
town and be worth his weight in gold, because right
now there is a shortage of good mayors in many
small villages.

HOOF
That is very well said and well thought. Let's call
Rock, may he enter and let's see how far goes his
genius.

PECAN (*announces them as the four peasants
enter*)
Smoke, Frog, Rock, Hamhock.
The four candidates have entered.
Here they are.

HOOF
Welcome gentlemen

ROCK
Well received, gentlemen.

CRUMB
Make yourself comfortable. We have plenty of
chairs.

SMOKE
I sit down and sitting I am.

HAMHOCK
We will all sit down, praise the lord.

FROG
What are you worried about, Smoke?

SMOKE
That the nomination is taking so long.
Should we buy the nomination with turkeys?
With jars of syrup, and leather flasks of old wine, so
full that they strain the stitches?
Just say it, and it will be solved quickly.

HOOF
There is no bribing here. We are all of the same
belief. The one who has the most abilities as mayor
will consider himself chosen and called to the
position.

FROG
That's fine, I am happy with that.

ROCK
I am happy with that, too.

HOOF
All in good time.

SMOKE
I am also happy with that.

HAMHOCK
I am pleasantly happy, also.

HOOF
Let us begin the test.

SMOKE
Bring on the test.

HOOF
Do you know how to read, Smoke?

SMOKE
I certainly do not. Nor will it be proven that there is anyone in my lineage that has such little status as to indulge in such illusions, that take men to the coals and women to a disorderly house. To read, I know

not. But I know other things that are more advantageous.

HOOF
What are they?

SMOKE
I know by heart all four prayers, and I pray them every week, four or five times.

FROG
And with that, you think you are qualified to be mayor?

SMOKE
With that, and with me being an old Christian, I even dare to become a Roman senator.

HOOF
That's very good. Hamhock, now you tell us what you know.

HAMHOCK
I, Mr. Hoof, know how to read—but not much. I know my letters and I have been learning B and A makes "Ba" for the last three months. Within the next five months I will be finished with that. Besides learning this "science," I know how to hook a plow properly and, in only three hours, I can brand four pairs of wild and lively calves.

I have all my limbs, I am not deaf, I have no cataracts, I do not cough and I have no rheumatism. I am, like everyone, an old Christian, and I draw a bow like King Tulio.

PECAN
Those are rare skills for a mayor—they are necessary and many.

HOOF
Moving on. What does Rock know?

ROCK
I have all my skills in my tongue and in my throat. There is not a liquid in the world that cannot reach me. There are sixty-six flavors engraved on my palate—all of them wines.

PECAN
And you want to be a mayor?

ROCK
I require it, because when I am armed, Bacchus style, my senses pick up. To the point, I believe at that point I could lend laws to Licurgo and clean myself with Bartulo.

CRUMB
Slow down! We're in council!

ROCK

I am not priggish at all, nor piggish. I only say, do not cross my way of justice or I will throw the whole wine cellar out the window.

HOOF

Threats here? By my life, Rock, here your threats are worthless. What does Peter Frog know?

FROG

As a frog, I should sing badly. But in spite of all this, I will talk about my condition and not my ingenuity. If I, my lords, were ever a mayor, my staff of office would not be as thin as the ones that are ordinarily used. I would make it out of oak and two fingers thick—afraid that it would bend under the sweet weight of the purse, full of coins, or bend under the weight of promises or favors that are as heavy as lead, that you don't feel until they have bruised the ribs of the body and the soul, and, together with this, I would be well mannered and cautious, partly severe but not at all strict. I will never dishonor the miserable man whose transgressions led him to be brought in front of me, because usually one word from a reckless judge hurts, because of the insult, much more than the weight of the sentence—even if it is a cruel punishment. It is not good if power precludes good breeding, nor if the submission of the delinquent makes the judge haughty and arrogant.

PECAN
Long life to God, that the Frog just sung much better
than a dying swan.

CRUMB
A thousand censoring sentences the frog has said.

PECAN
From Caton censoring. Crumb has spoken well.

CRUMB
Reproach me.

PECAN
The time will come.

SNEEZE
Let's hope the time never comes. Your reproaches,
Pecan, are a terrible inclination.

PECAN
No more, you scribe.

SNEEZE
What scribe, Pharisee?

HOOF
By St. Peter, this is too much.

PECAN
I was just joking.

SNEEZE
I am also joking.

HOOF
No more jokes, for my life.

PECAN
He who lies, lies.

SNEEZE
He who says the truth, says the truth.

PECAN
True.

SNEEZE
Then everybody close your mouths.

SMOKE
Those offerings that Frog made are from far away. I believe that if he holds the mace he will change and become a different man from what he seems like now.

HOOF
What Smoke says fits the mold.

SMOKE
And I will add more: that if they give me the mace,
they will see how I will not transform, I will not
turn, I will not change.

HOOF
Here is the mace and pretend that you are already
mayor.

PECAN
Body of the world! Do they give him a left-handed
mace.

SMOKE
What do you mean left handed?

PECAN
Isn't it left handed, this mace? A deaf or a mute
could see that from a distance.

SMOKE
How, if they give me a left-handed mace, do they
want me to judge right?

SNEEZE
This Pecan has the devil inside his body. Where has
anybody ever before seen left-handed maces?

(*Uno enters*)

UNO
Gentlemen, there are here some gypsies with some miraculous little gypsy girls. And even though they have been told that your excellencies are occupied, they keep insisting that they enter to give you solace, my lords.

HOOF
Let them enter and we will see if they can be useful for the holiday of Corpus Christi of which I am the organizer.

CRUMB
Good, let them enter in good time.

ROCK
Let them enter.

SMOKE
As for me, I already wish they were here.

HAMHOCK
For me, in a jiffy!

FROG
Aren't they gypsies? Then you all be careful they will not steal our noses.

UNO
Without calling them, they come. They are already inside.

(*Enter musicians dressed as gypsies with two well-dressed gypsy girls. The males sing while the girls dance.*)

Song:
>   The body bows to you all
>   Councilors of Daganzo
>   Good men suddenly
>   Good men of thought
>   Of good judgment forewarned
>   To provide the positions
>   That ambition requires
>   Between Moors and Christians.
>   It seems that the heavens have made you,
>   I mean, the starry skies.
>   Sampsons for the letters
>   And for the strengths, Bártulos.

HAMHOCK
Everything that is sung refers to history.

SMOKE
The girls and the boys are unique and thin.

PECAN
They have something thick about them.

HOOF
Ah! Suffice. Enough.

Song:
>As the winds change,
>As the branches change,
>That nude in winter,
>Dress in the summer,
>We will change our dances,
>By points and in each step,
>Since the fact that women change
>Is not new or strange

ALL
Long live the rulers of Daganzo, that look like palm trees because they are oaks.

HAMHOCK
Great song, by God.

SMOKE
And with great feeling.

ROCK
It should be published so the memory of us all will remain forever and ever, amen.

HOOF
Be quiet, if you can.

Song:
> Long life and re-long life.
> And in the speedy centuries
> Of time, the days
> Pass with the nights,
> Without changing age
> That thirty years form,
> Nor touching the leaves of
> Your cork trees.
> The winds that flood
> When running contrary,
> Will change to soft zephyrs
> When blowing in your seas.

ALL
Long live the rulers of Daganzo that look like palm trees because they are oaks.

HOOF
Parts of the refrain displease me, but as a whole, it is good.

ROCK
Ha! Let's be quiet.

Song:
> I will step on the dust
> That is so thin

(*All sing*)
Step on the dust
That is so fine.

CRUMB
These musicians, they make a hodge-podge of their
song

SMOKE
They are devils, these gypsies.

Song:
> I will step on the ground
> No matter how hard it is,
> So Love will open
> A grave for me,
> Since already my good fortune
> Was stomped by Love.

(*All sing*)
> That is so fine!

GIRL
> I will step lushly
> On the hardest ground,
> If, by chance, you step on it,
> You might step on bad things I fear.
> My good fortune will pass in a flash.

(*All sing*)
> And he left the dust
> That is so fine.

(*The church keeper enters, he is in a bad mood*).

FRIAR
Gentlemen rulers. I swear to Dico! Villanous rogues, so much entertainment. Is this the way a village should be ruled? In bad hours of guitars, dances and amusements?

HOOF
Catch him, Hamhock.

HAMHOCK
I will catch him.

HOOF
Bring here a blanket in which, by Christ, we should toss this rogue, impertinent, shameless, insolent — and, on top of that, bold.

FRIAR
Listen, gentlemen.

PECAN
I will return with the blanket in a flash

(*He leaves*)

FRIAR
See that I tell you, I am a friar.

HOOF
You, a priest, scoundrel?

FRIAR
Yes, a friar, or from the first tonsure [He points to
his monk-shaved head], which is the same.

CRUMB
Now you will see, said Agrajes the knight.

FRIAR
There is no Agrajes here.

CRUMB
Then there will be grackles that will peck your
tongue and your eyes.

FROG
Tell me, wretch, what demon got wrapped around
your tongue? Who orders you to scold the justices?
Are you going to govern the republic? Mind your
bells and your business. Leave alone those who
govern, because they know what they must do better
than we do. If they were bad, pray for their amends;
if they were good, pray God will not take them from
us.

HOOF
Our Frog is a saint and a blessed one.

(*Pecan returns with a blanket*)

PECAN
It's not for the lack of a blanket.

HOOF
Grab it then, all, including the gypsies. Up with him, friends!

(*They put him on the blanket and toss him up.*)

FRIAR
My God, they are serious. God forgive me if I get upset, for I am not good with these sorts of jokes. For St. Peter, everyone who has touched even a hair of the blanket is excommunicated!

FROG
Stop! No more. Let the punishment stop here—the poor man must be repentant.

FRIAR
And beaten down, which is more. From now on I will sew my mouth with shoemaker's laces.

FROG
That's what is important.

HOOF
Let the gypsies come to my house because I have to
tell them something.

GYPSIES
After you.

HOOF
So the election will be postponed until tomorrow,
And I will give my vote to Frog.

GYPSIES
Shall we sing, sir?

HOOF
Whatever you want.

CRUMB
Nobody sings like our Frog sings.

HAMHOCKS
Not only does he chant, but he also enchants.

(*All exit singing*)

     I will step on the dust
     That is so fine...

End.

www.ingramcontent.com/pod-product-compliance
Lightning Source LLC
Chambersburg PA
CBHW041720090426
42739CB00019B/3490